A GIFT FOR

Dear Maurice,
who has such a
gift for friendship.

÷ FROM ÷

Helen
with love and
appreciation.

OTHER GIFTBOOKS BY HELEN EXLEY:
In Praise and Celebration of Friends
The Love Between Sisters
Thank you for Every Little Thing
Words on Kindness
Words on the Power of Friendship
Words on Love and Caring
The Love Between Mothers and Daughters
A Little Book for a Friend

Published simultaneously in 2000 by Exley Publications LLC in the USA and Exley Publications Ltd in Great Britain.

12 11 10 9 8 7 6 5 4 3

ISBN 1-86187-199-6

Edited and pictures selected by Helen Exley.
Pictures researched by Image Select International.
Printed in China.

**Exley Publications Ltd, 16 Chalk Hill, Watford,
Herts WD19 4BG, UK.
Exley Publications LLC, 185 Main Street, Spencer,
MA 01562, USA.
www.helenexleygiftbooks.com**

THE LOVE
BETWEEN
FRIENDS

A HELEN EXLEY GIFTBOOK

EXLEY

THE POWER OF TWO

*I'm not strong. She's not strong.
But together my friend
and I make the strongest force
in the known universe.*

LINDA MACFARLANE

*The world is so wide and each of
us so small – yet bound by
friendship we are giants.*

PAM BROWN, b.1928

Friends are together
when they are separated,
they are rich when they are poor,
strong when they are weak, and –
a thing even harder to explain –
they live on after they have died,
so great is the honour that follows
them, so vivid
the memory, so poignant
the sorrow.

CICERO (106-43 B.C.)

... the finest thing of all about
friendship is that it sends a ray of
good hope into the future, and
keeps our hearts from faltering
or falling to the wayside.

CICERO (106-43 B.C.)

When a friend asks
there is no tomorrow.

GEORGE HERBERT (1593-1633)

There are many routes into a person's heart
which make you a treasured friend.
Each act of kindness. Each moment shared.
Each word of praise or comfort. These are
the ways – the paths, which through time
become highways, along which lie
the journey of friendship.

STUART AND LINDA MACFARLANE

*Friends have a unique
loyalty to one another.
This loyalty comes not
through a sense of duty
in the way one may show
loyalty to family, kinsfolk or
country. Theirs is born out
of love, trust and respect.
Nurtured on care and
understanding.
A perfect loyalty that will
survive every hardship
and endure the rigorous
test of time.*

STUART AND LINDA
MACFARLANE

PUTTING UP WITH
EACH OTHER

Friends have come to an agreement.
You put up with my idiosyncrasies.
I'll put up with yours.

She's jolly insulting. If anyone else
said the things she says,
I'd... She's usually right, of course,
and the best thing is that I can take
any insult from her because I know
she's on my side.

JENNY DE VRIES

UNDERSTANDING
EACH OTHER

To know someone with whom
you feel there is understanding
in spite of distances or thoughts
unexpressed — that can make of this
earth a garden.

JOHANN WOLFGANG VON GOETHE
(1749-1832)

I love you because you have done
more than any creed could have
done to make me good, and more
than any fate could have done to
make me happy.

You have done it without a touch,
without a word, without a sign.

You have done it by being yourself.
Perhaps that is what being a friend
means after all.

ROY CROFT

Deft thieves can break your locks
and carry off your savings,
fire consume your home...
fortune can't take away
what you give friends:
that wealth stays yours forever.

MARCUS MARTIAL (c.40-c.104)

Friend, whatever hardships threaten
If thou call me,
I'll befriend thee,
All-enduring, fearlessly,
I'll befriend thee.

OGLALA SIOUX INDIAN

We've been friends forever.
I suppose that can't be true.
There must have been a time
before we became friends
but I can't remember it.
You are in my first memory
and all my best memories
ever since.

LINDA MACFARLANE

No one can give you back
your youth. But with an old
friend, you never lose it.

PAM BROWN, b.1928

GOOD TIMES

*It is the small,
insignificant, simple
gestures that make life
bearable. A smile,
a touch, a word,
a kindness, a concern.*

PAM BROWN, b.1928

*Grief can take care of
itself, but to get the full
value of joy, you must
have a friend with
whom to share it.*

KAHLIL GIBRAN (1883-1931)

*Friends... like to make
you feel great. That's...
what friends are for.*

CELIA BRAYFIELD,
FROM "WOMAN AND HOME",
OCTOBER 1997

FRIENDSHIP IS BASED ON
CHEMISTRY AND TRUST...
AND WHY IT HAPPENS OR
WHY IT RISES AND FALLS, AND
RISES AGAIN, IS A MYSTERY,
LIKE A FINE PIECE OF MUSIC.

RICHARD LOUV,
FROM "THE WEB OF LIFE"

FRIENDSHIP COMES WITH
LONG ACQUAINTANCE — OR
IN A SUDDEN SMILE.
FRIENDSHIP IS DEEP-ROOTED
AS AN OAK OR LIGHT AND
LOVELY AS A BIRD.

PAM BROWN, b.1928

... no one ever told me what a wonderful thing friendship would be. I remember... lying in my best friend's garden feeling exquisitely happy just to be with her. We were discovering the world together, making up the rules for ourselves, creating our own little universe of tastes, preferences and morals. And jokes. Remember laughing out of control about absolutely nothing? We did lots of that.

CELIA BRAYFIELD,
FROM "WOMAN AND HOME", OCTOBER 1997

SOMEONE TO TRUST

With a person I trust I can tell her
all my problems without anyone
knowing. I can tell her
all my secrets like a secret diary.

PRIYA PATEL, AGE 10

SOMEONE WHO UNDERSTANDS

The friends who listen to us
are the ones we move toward,
and we want to sit in their radius.
When we are listened to,
it creates us, makes us unfold
and expand.

KARL MENNINGER
(1893-1990)

*One's friends are
that part of the
human race with
which one can
be human.*

GEORGE SANTAYANA
(1863-1952)

*Oh, the comfort –
the inexpressible
comfort, of feeling safe
with a person – having
neither to weigh
thoughts nor measure
words, but pouring
them all right out....*

DINAH MARIA MULOCK CRAIK
(1826-1887)

A friend's writing on an envelope
lifts the heart on the rainiest
morning.

CHARLOTTE GRAY

There are no goodbyes for us.
Wherever you are, you will always
be in my heart.

MAHATMA GANDHI (1869-1948)

A friend may move away – so far
that you may never meet again.
And yet they are a part of you
forever.

PAM BROWN, b.1928

Those special friends
whom I am closest to...
interest me: how they think,
what they feel, how they
deal with life – its gifts
and its denials. They add
to and complete
the circle of my life
and enrich me.
They are
what I hang onto.

LAUREN BACALL, b.1924,
FROM "NOW"

To others, we will be seen as two old biddies kicking off their shoes, dumping down shopping bags, choosing lethal pastries. But to each other we are ourselves, a little scarred by the passing years, but still the girls who shared a bag of toffee on the playground wall, we at least are not deceived by skin, spectacles and silvery hair.

PAM BROWN, b.1928

Old friends disintegrate together – which enlivens the process.

PAM BROWN, b.1928

BETWEEN TWO PEOPLE

There was nothing remote or mysterious here – only something private. The only secret was the ancient communication between two people.

EUDORA WELTY, b.1909

A million billion words have been spoken about what friendship means but two good friends can be together without speaking a single word and know precisely what friendship means.

STUART AND LINDA MACFARLANE

*Like the shade of a great tree
in the noonday heat is a friend.
Like the home port with your
country's flag flying after
a long journey is a friend.
A friend is an impregnable
citadel of refuge in the strife
of existence.*

AUTHOR UNKNOWN

*The most I can do for my friend
is simply to be his friend. I have
no wealth to bestow upon him.
If he knows that I am happy
in loving him he will want
no other reward.
Is not friendship divine in this?*

LAVATIN

Friends are there when your
hopes are ravelled
and your nerves are knotted,
talking about nothing in
particular, you can feel
the tangles untwist.

PAM BROWN, b.1928

My friend and I tell each other
all our worries. Often there is
nothing we can do to solve
them. But knowing that we are
there for each other, prepared
to listen, is all the help we need.

LINDA MACFARLANE

*One can do without
people, but one has
need of a friend.*

CHINESE PROVERB

*In prosperity our
friends know us;
In adversity we know
our friends.*

J.M. BARRIE (1860-1937)

*When chill winds blow
fierce, a friend acts like
a torch, guiding you
to safety, giving you
warmth, comforting you
till the storm is over.*

STUART AND LINDA
MACFARLANE

I love you
for closing your ears
to the discords in me,
and for adding to the music
in me by wonderful listening.
I love you because you are
helping me to make of...
the words of my every day
not a reproach, but a song.

ROY CROFT

Then little by little we
discover one friend, in
the midst of the crowd
of friends, who is
particularly happy to
be with us and to
whom, we realize,
we have an infinite
number of things
to say.

NATALIA GINZBURG, b.1916,
FROM "THE LITTLE VIRTUES"

Some people come
into our lives and
quickly go...
Some people stay for
a while and leave their
footprints on our
hearts, and we are
never, ever the same.

FLAVIA

The greatest healing therapy
is friendship and love.

HUBERT HUMPHREY
(1911-1978)

So long as we love we serve;
so long as we are loved by
others, I would almost say
that we are indispensable;
and no man is useless while
he has a friend.

ROBERT LOUIS STEVENSON
(1850-1894)

What seems to
grow fairer to me
as life goes by is
the love and the
grace and
tenderness of it;
not its wit and
cleverness and
grandeur of
knowledge – grand
as knowledge is –
but just the
laughter of
children and the
friendship of
friends, and the
cozy talk by the
fire, and the sight
of flowers, and the
sound of music.

AUTHOR UNKNOWN

MY OLD FRIENDS

Long friendships are like jewels,
polished over time to become
beautiful and enduring.

CELIA BRAYFIELD,
FROM "WOMAN AND HOME",
OCTOBER 1997

I have had many friends that time
and distance, change and loss have
swept away. I hold their memory,
flowers pressed between the days –
and breathing still the scent
of distant summers.
But some remain – deep-rooted in my
life and bright with living blossom.
A constant comfort and
a constant joy.

PAM BROWN, b.1928

Ah, how good it feels!
The hand of an old friend!

HENRY WADSWORTH LONGFELLOW
(1807-1882)

THE BEST OF LIFE

I love Cara and you with unchanged
and unchangeable affection, and while
I retain your friendship I retain the best
that life has given me next to that which
is the deepest and gravest joy in all
human experience.

GEORGE ELIOT (MARY ANN EVANS)
(1819-1880)

I count your friendship one of the chief
pleasures of my life, a comfort
in time of doubt and trouble, a joy in
time of prosperity and success,
and an inspiration at all times.

EDWIN O. GROVER

She became for me an island
of light, fun, and wisdom where
I could run with my discoveries
and torments and hopes
at any time of the day
and find welcome.

MAY SARTON

Two people, yes, two lasting friends,
The giving comes, the taking ends.
There is no measure for such things,
For this all Nature slows and sings.

ELIZABETH JENNINGS, b.1926,
FROM "FRIENDSHIP"

ACKNOWLEDGEMENTS: The publishers are grateful for permission to reproduce copyright material. Whilst every reasonable effort has been made to trace copyright holders, the publishers would be pleased to hear from any not here acknowledged. ELIZABETH JENNINGS: From *"Friendship"* from *New Poems 1970-71*, ed. Alan Brownjohn, Seamus Heaney and Joan Stallworthy. Published by Hutchinson.

PICTURE CREDITS: Exley Publications is very grateful to the following organizations and individuals for permission to reproduce their pictures. Whilst all efforts have been made to clear copyright and acknowledge sources and artists, we would be happy to hear from any copyright holder who may have been omitted. AISA; Archiv für Kunst (AKG); Art Resource (AR); The Bridgeman Art Library (BAL); Edimedia (EDI); Fine Art Photographic Library (FAP); Giraudon (GIR); National Museum of American Art (NMAA); Superstock (SS). Cover: © 2000 Frederick Stead, *Poppies*, BAL; title page: © 2000 Martha Walter, *Ladies Knitting*, SS; p.7: August Macke, *Girls under Trees*, private collection; pp.8/9: Peter Severin Kroyer, *Summer Evening at the South Beach, Skagen*, BAL; p.10: William-Adolphe Bouguereau, *The Nut Gatherer*, BAL; p.12: Pierre Auguste Renoir, *Bal du Moulin de la Galette, Montmartre*, Lauros-Giraudon; p.14: © 2000 Gebhard Bondzin, *Annemarie*, AKG; p.16: © 2000 William Percy Gibbs, *Interior Scene with Two Ladies*, BAL; p.18: Peder Severin Kroyer, *Boys on the Beach, at Skagen*, EDI; pp.20/21: Lev Felixovitch Lagorio, *Beside the Sea*, GIR; p.23: Sir Francis Bernard Dicksee, *Old Songs*, FAP; p.25: © 2000 Andrew Macara, *Reaching for Oranges, Bentota, Sri Lanka*, BAL; p.26: © 2000 William Stewart MacGeorge, *Sloe Blossom*, BAL; pp.28/29: © 2000 Dame Laura Knight, *Young Gypsies*, BAL; p.30: Camille Pissarro, *The Chatterer*, private collection; p.32: © 2000 Edmond Verstraeten, *Daughters*, SS; p.35: William Kay Blacklock, *The Letter*, BAL; p.36: Irving Ramsey Wiles, *Russian Tea*, NMAA; p.38: © 2000 Gillian Lawson, *At the Seaside*, BAL; pp.40/41: Thomas Wilmer Dewing, *The Hermit Thrush*, AR; p.42: © 2000 T. Wieghardt, *Knitting*, SS; p.45: © 2000 Richard Emil Miller, *The Dressing Table*, SS; p.46: Bunny, *The Conversation*, GIR; p.48: © 2000 Antonio Ko, Jr, *The Basket Weavers*, private collection; p.50: Peter Hansen, *Little Girls Playing*, EDI; p.52: © 2000 William Harold Dudley, *The Summer Cottage*, BAL; p.55: © 2000 Thomas Cantrell Dugdale, *A Caller, Candlelight and Tea*, BAL; p.57: Albert Gustaf Edelfelt, *Meeting outside the Church*, AISA; p.58: August Macke, *Four Girls*, SS; pp.60/61: Pierre Auguste Renoir, *The Skiff*, BAL.